**B**

Time-saving books that teach specific skills to busy people, focusing on what really matters; the things that make a difference – the *essentials*. Other books in the series include:

**Create Great Spreadsheets**

**The Ultimate Business Plan**

**Speaking in Public**

**Responding to Stress**

**Succeeding at Interviews**

**Solving Problems**

**Hiring People**

**Getting Started on the Internet**

**Writing Business E-mails**

**Making the Best Man's Speech**

**Making Great Presentations**

**Making the Most of Your Time**

For full details please send for a free copy of the latest catalogue. See back cover for address.

*The things that really matter about*

# Buying a Franchise

**Phil Stone**

**ESSENTIALS**

Published in 2001 by
How To Books Ltd, 3 Newtec Place,
Magdalen Road, Oxford OX4 1RE, United Kingdom
Tel: (01865) 793806    Fax: (01865) 248780
e-mail: info@howtobooks.co.uk
www.howtobooks.co.uk

British Library Cataloguing in Publication Data.
A catalogue record for this book is available from
the British Library.

Edited by Diana Brueton
Cover design by Shireen Nathoo Design
Produced for How To Books by Deer Park Productions
Typeset by PDQ Typesetting, Newcastle-under-Lyme, Staffordshire
Printed and bound by Baskerville Press, Salisbury, Wiltshire

NOTE: The material contained in this book is set out in good faith for
general guidance and no liability can be accepted for loss or expense
incurred as a result of relying in particular circumstances on
statements made in the book. Laws and regulations are complex
and liable to change, and readers should check the current position
with the relevant authorities before making personal arrangements.

**ESSENTIALS** *is an imprint of*
**How To Books**

# Contents

# Preface

If you are considering starting your own business you could look at the option of buying a franchise. In plain terms a franchise is a business that has already been tested in the market and proven to be a success. You must understand, however, that it is the concept that has been proven and that by itself will not guarantee success for you.

Franchising is really an informal partnership. The franchisor will want to ensure that your business is launched successfully and that it remains profitable. Their income as well as yours will depend on your success. This creates a bond between the two parties in terms of a close dependence on each other.

Buying a franchise will allow you to run your own business, but unlike a new start-up business you will have the ongoing help and assistance from the franchisor to make it a success.

As with all businesses there will be risks but a franchise should reduce those risks. Statistically the number of business failures relating to franchises is far less than those relating to new start-up businesses.

Franchising is not an easy option. It can, however, make running your own business a lot easier.

*Phil Stone*

# 1 The Concept of Franchising

*A franchise is not an easy option. It may, however, give a better overall chance of success than starting your own business.*

## 4

**things that really matter**

1 **UNDERSTANDING A FRANCHISE**

2 **CONSIDERING THE BENEFITS**

3 **ACCEPTING THE DISADVANTAGES**

4 **KNOWING THE DIFFERENT TYPES OF FRANCHISE**

The whole concept of franchising is not new. It was originally conceived in America as a way to expand a business operation without increasing overhead cost. Since the early 1970s franchising has become more and more popular in the UK. According to a survey published by the British Franchise Association in 2000, the market has nearly 642 different franchise operations that are now worth in excess of £8.9bn. Franchised businesses include McDonalds and Burger King, but franchising is not just confined to fast food outlets.

Franchises cover a wide range of business areas and at varying prices from a few thousand up to hundreds of thousands of pounds. Differences in the quality and background of a franchise mean you need to exercise great care when considering a purchase. From the outset check with the British Franchise Association (BFA) that the franchise you are looking at is a member. The BFA accredit their members against a wide range of criteria and you are strongly advised to consider only an accredited franchise.

### IS THIS YOU?

 • *I've heard about franchising but don't know what it is.* • *How do I go about finding a suitable franchise?* • *What advantages are there in buying a franchise?* • *With a proven business concept how can there be any disadvantages?*

*Buying a business idea that has already been tried and tested is a safer way of starting your own business. It is, however, not necessarily a recipe for your own success and you will still have to work hard to achieve prosperity.*

### ① UNDERSTANDING A FRANCHISE

First, for the avoidance of doubt, a **franchisor** refers to the seller of the franchise and the **franchisee** refers to the purchaser of the franchise.

In simplistic terms a franchise is a *licence granted by one person to another* to use a business idea in a defined format. There is, however, a formal definition that has been set out by the British Franchise Association. The pertinent parts are as follows.

A franchise is a contractual licence granted by one person (the franchisor) to another (the franchisee) which:

- Permits or requires the franchisee to carry on, during the period of the franchise, a particular business under or using a specified name belonging to or associated with the franchisor;
- Entitles the franchisor to exercise continuing control during the period of the franchise over the manner in which the franchisee carries on the business which is the subject of the franchise;

- Obliges the franchisor to provide the franchisee with assistance in carrying on the business which is the subject of the franchise (in relation to the organisation of the franchisee's business, the training of staff, merchandising, management or otherwise);
- Requires the franchisee periodically during the period of the franchise to pay to the franchisor sums of money in consideration for the franchise or for goods or services provided by the franchisor to the franchisee.

Whilst this definition concentrates on the concept of a franchise it does not deal with the practical elements. For example, it makes no reference to the *initial training* that will be required for the establishment of the franchise. It also does not mention the requirement for an *initial capital investment* that will be required from you. Both of these form an integral part of the franchise concept.

Taking all these factors into consideration, a franchise is therefore a business relationship between the franchisor, who has a tried and tested business concept, and yourself who purchases the right to operate a branded business. It will involve a capital investment in addition to ongoing *royalty or management fees* either based on sales turnover or as a mark-up on goods supplied for resale by the franchisor.

The franchisor will provide initial training in all aspects of the franchise in order to ensure that you are equipped to run the franchise successfully. The franchisor will also provide ongoing assistance and support to you in all aspects of the franchise operation.

*A franchise is a successful business concept with proven marketing and operational methods. It means that you are in business for yourself but you are not on your own. You have the constant support and guidance of the franchisor in the background.*

**CONSIDERING THE BENEFITS**

There are clear and obvious benefits in buying a franchise, the most important of which is that, as already stated, you will be purchasing a *tried and tested business concept*. It may not be cheaper than starting your own business in the same sort of market but it does bring with it a recognised brand image. It is estimated that whilst only one in five new-start businesses will still be trading after five years, some 90 per cent of franchise operations will have succeeded.

There are numerous benefits in buying a franchise, some of which are:

- You will have the opportunity to purchase a business concept that has already been tried and tested in the market.
- The risks of setting up a franchised business are substantially reduced when compared to establishing a new business in the same market.
- A franchise will provide a brand image that the public will recognise.
- Business premises will all comply with an established interior and exterior design to assist with brand promotion.
- Specifications for the equipment required by the franchise will be clearly identified from the outset.
- Publicity and ongoing marketing can be arranged by the franchisor as part of the contractual agreement.
- Comprehensive training in all aspects of running the business will be given to you by the franchisor, both initially and on an ongoing basis as methods are improved.
- The 'operations manual' received as part of the franchise

will give standardised procedures for accounting, sales and stock control.

- The franchisor may be able to provide you with better terms for the centralised bulk purchase of raw materials or goods used by the franchise.
- As the franchisee, you should benefit from the franchisor's ongoing research and development undertaken to improve the franchised product or service.
- Networking with other franchisees will provide both you and the franchisor with opportunities for review and improvement of the operating procedures.
- The franchise should have a clearly defined geographical area within which the rights of the franchise are protected from other franchises from the same franchisor.

## Raising funds for the venture

The final advantage of purchasing a franchise, as opposed to starting your own business, relates to *raising funding* for the venture. Gaining finance to purchase a franchise is generally easier than gaining finance to start a new business. The reason for this is that the franchisor will be better able to provide estimates of the likely sales and costs, thereby giving a more accurate prediction of profit levels.

Most of the high street banks have specialist franchise sections that monitor the ongoing progress of their franchise customers. In this way they build up a picture of the success or otherwise of a franchise and, whilst they will not pass on an opinion as to ongoing viability, they will obviously be more prepared to finance a franchise that has a successful history.

It may well be, therefore, that if you are having difficulty obtaining finance for the purchase of a franchise you should perhaps be looking at it more carefully. Under some circumstances the franchisor may be able to offer assistance with funding. A well established franchisor will often make arrangements with a particular bank to fund the purchase of a franchise. You as franchisee will still have responsibility for the loan, but the involvement of the franchisor may increase the likelihood that the loan will be granted.

 **ACCEPTING THE DISADVANTAGES**

As with all business ventures there are of course some disadvantages to buying a franchise. Being a franchisee means that you are buying a *total business concept* and there is subsequently no room for individuality in terms of the product or service offered. The franchisor will demand that all aspects of the business are operated exactly as set out in the operations manual, with uniform standards for appearance and packaging of the goods or services.

Many prospective franchisees consider that they can improve on the way that things are done. That may well be the case, but unless the franchisor agrees you will be forced to conduct your business exactly as they tell you.

Once a franchise has been purchased it can be difficult to dispose of as there are often limitations placed on any re-sale. The franchisor will, more than likely, want to approve the potential purchaser in addition to which they will probably want some control over the sale price.

### Other disadvantages

It can also be extremely difficult to enforce exclusive *territory rights*. When you purchase a franchise the franchisor will usually undertake not to sell another franchise within a defined geographical area. Whilst the franchisor would be unwise to break the terms of the franchise agreement in this respect, there is of course nothing to stop customers from obtaining the same goods or services from another franchisee in a neighbouring territory.

Disputes over the *royalty fee or management charge* that is usually based on sales turnover or profits are not uncommon. As part of the contractual agreement the franchisor will normally undertake centralised marketing campaigns, the lack of which will undoubtedly have an impact on sales. By the same token, it could be that the franchisor undertakes marketing campaigns that have little benefit for a particular franchisee in, say, a remote location.

Another cause of disputes over the royalty fee based on sales turnover is the question of *special promotions*. With the income of the franchisor from you depending on volume of turnover they may not be concerned with your overall profitability. Whilst this is a rather short-sighted attitude it is possible for the franchisor to insist upon price cuts or special offers that will increase turnover, and therefore their royalty fee, at the expense of your profitability.

As well as the royalty fee you may be forced, under the terms of the franchise, to only buy *goods and services* from the franchisor. Apart from the fact that these could be at disadvantageous prices it should be remembered that the franchisor will also normally have control over the selling price. This effectively gives the franchisor the right to control overall profit margins.

The final disadvantage is the possibility that *the franchisor may fail*, leaving you with a business that may not be viable in isolation.

*The point to remember is that the franchisor will place all manner of controls and obligations on you. The possibility of you controlling the actions of the franchisor are, however, minimal.*

If the franchisor receives bad publicity this will affect the whole brand or image of the franchise and therefore every individual franchisee.

 **KNOWING THE DIFFERENT TYPES OF FRANCHISE**

Franchising opportunities are available for all sorts of businesses in all manner of markets; provided the original concept can be replicated it may be suitable to be franchised. In order to assess whether a business is suitable for a potential franchise there are a number of criteria that you will need to consider:

- The original business concept must have been tried and tested and proved to be a success.
- The franchise should be capable of a distinct brand image in addition to having standardised systems and methods.
- The systems and methods must be capable of being clearly defined within an operations manual so as to transfer this knowledge to you.
- Operation of the franchise must provide you with sufficient profitability to reward you for the original investment and ongoing work.
- The franchise also needs to generate sufficient income for the franchisor in terms of the sale of the original business concept and the ongoing income from management fees or royalties.

When deciding whether a business is capable of being operated as a franchise it is obviously necessary for you to consider the characteristics of the business. In some ways it is easier to consider the potential by looking at the characteristics that could render a business unsuitable for franchising. These could include:

- Products that have a very short life span in the market.
- Businesses with minimal profitability.
- Services that require considerable training to reach the required skill level.
- Businesses with repeat business based on loyalty to an individual rather than a product or service.
- Businesses that are only specific to one geographical area.

In summary, there are no real boundaries to franchising most business concepts providing they meet the basic criteria for a franchise. Franchising can be an excellent opportunity for you to run your own business using an original successful concept with proven marketing and operating methods. A successful franchise is really a partnership between you, as the franchisee, and the franchisor who will provide ongoing support behind the scenes.

**KEY POINTS**

✓ Contact the British Franchise Association for assistance in locating a suitable franchise or to check that your proposed franchisor is a member.

✓ Purchasing a franchise has clear advantages over starting a brand new business in the same market.

✓ Funding the purchase of a franchise can be a lot easier than obtaining finance for a yet to be proven business venture.

✓ Be aware of the pitfalls – a franchise is a proven business concept but there can also be many disadvantages.

# 2 Selecting a Franchise

*Buying a franchise can involve a large investment. The selection process must therefore be thorough and wide-ranging.*

**3**

**things that really matter**

1 **ESTABLISHING WHAT IS BEING OFFERED**

2 **RESEARCHING THE BACKGROUND**

3 **OBTAINING A SECOND OPINION**

You must understand exactly *what sort of franchise* you are looking for before deciding and also *how much you can invest* towards the purchase cost and *how much, if necessary, you can afford to borrow*. Purchasing a franchise is a major investment and careful selection is vital for success.

A prime consideration is whether you are capable of starting your own business in the same market. The added protection that a franchise can offer to you will only apply if you have existing knowledge of the market. For example, you will not become a skilled motor mechanic solely by purchasing a franchise. Prior experience is essential.

When looking at the suitability of a franchise you must also consider the market. In a declining market, a franchise will only offer a small advantage over starting your own business. Look at the *overall picture* and not just the past performance of a franchise when making a selection. Whether it is a franchise or not there must be additional market opportunities for your new business to succeed.

**IS THIS YOU?**

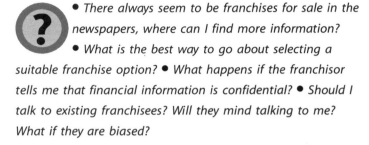

• *There always seem to be franchises for sale in the newspapers, where can I find more information?*
• *What is the best way to go about selecting a suitable franchise option?* • *What happens if the franchisor tells me that financial information is confidential?* • *Should I talk to existing franchisees? Will they mind talking to me? What if they are biased?*

### ① ESTABLISHING WHAT IS BEING OFFERED

Apart from the British Franchise Association, a good source of information on available franchises can be obtained from *Franchise World*. They are the publishers of *Franchise World Magazine* and also the *Annual Franchise Directory*.

When selecting a franchise you need to be clear about exactly what it is you are being offered and what form of franchise it is. There are three types of franchise:

- **Job franchise** – effectively you are purchasing a job for yourself. The capital investment required will usually range from £5,000 up to £20,000 and these franchises take the form of single person businesses. Examples include mobile car mechanics and domestic carpet or fabric cleaners.
- **Business franchise** – these involve the purchase of a complete business that will require additional staff over and above your own involvement. Prices for this type of franchise range from £20,000 to £100,000. Examples include fast food operations and printing shops.
- **Investment franchise** – at the top of the scale and usually involving a substantial investment in excess of £100,000 with some costing as much as £1m. As would be expected there are few franchises in this price range.

Examples include hotels and restaurants. The vast majority of the franchise investment cost in these cases will be for the property and equipment required.

From the above you will see that it is easy to establish exactly what type of franchise you are being offered. What is sometimes more difficult to establish is exactly what you are being offered as part of the deal. For example, taking the case of a mobile mechanic, does the franchise fee include a customised vehicle and all equipment? Understanding *what you get for your money* is an extremely important aspect and is covered in greater detail in Chapter 4.

For the time being, however, you need to concentrate on the franchising concept that is on offer to you. You need to be absolutely certain that the market in which the franchise operates is thriving. As with all businesses, there will be a level of market penetration above which further expansion, using the same product or service, will not be feasible.

**Doing essential research**

For this reason you need to undertake a full analysis of the target market and research the trends within that market. If the franchise that you are considering has a single product or service you must establish that the product or service has developed over time and remains up to date. Remember, there will still be competitors to a franchise operation and you need to make suitable comparisons. In some cases there may even be rival competitor franchise operations in the same market. A good example of this would be the franchises operated by Kall Kwik and Prontaprint, both of which are in the printing market.

You must not be under the impression that the franchisor will answer all of these questions for you. It is vitally important that you do your own research as though you were starting your own business within the market. The franchisor cannot and will not guarantee your success.

*You may be buying a franchise, which makes starting up a lot easier, but you are still taking the risk.*

On a final note, you must also be aware that some so-called franchisors are not actually offering a franchise at all. As with all other aspects of business, there are potential fraudsters in the market and you need to be on your guard. Before you make any initial decisions on a prospective franchise you must always *obtain references*. You should also contact the British Franchise Association to establish whether the franchise you are considering are members. If they are not then you need to ask why not and whether they intend applying in due course.

Also talk to your bank. They have specialists who deal with franchising and they can offer specific help and guidance in making a selection. The decision will, of course, rest with you but *wide research* is required before you make a final choice.

*Buying a franchise is no different from buying any other business. The investigations that you undertake into the business concept and background must be just as thorough. You must treat the purchase as if you were investing your money in your own new start business. The risks and rewards of success are still the same.*

 **RESEARCHING THE BACKGROUND**

Having now made an initial decision on the franchise that you are interested in this is the time to refine your *research*

*into the franchisor.* At this stage, rather than limit yourself to one potential franchise I would recommend that you have a short list of at least two, preferably three. It will obviously depend on the type of business that you are looking at and the number of alternative franchisors available. In this way you will be able to make comparisons of performance in the market.

There are a number of factors that you need to be satisfied with when looking at the background to the franchise:

- You must obtain a detailed history of the background and development of the business including details of the number of pilot operations.
- You must establish how the business has expanded. How many franchises were in operation a year ago as opposed to the number now? What is the growth rate envisaged for the next five years?
- From the number of original franchises granted you need to establish how many are still trading. You also need to know how many have not survived, and how many have terminated their franchise contract. If the contract has been terminated try to establish the exact reasons.
- You must investigate the support services that will be available. If the franchise is expanding considerably you need to establish that the franchisor is able to cope with such expansion.
- You should enquire into the training methods used and establish exactly when training will be undertaken. Will it be given before you commence trading or is it given on an ongoing basis once you open for business?
- Establish the promotion methods used and the number

of advertising campaigns carried out in the last 12
months.

- You must also ensure that the products or services are
  being constantly reviewed by the franchisor and
  developed to meet the changing needs in the market.
  Ask for details of exactly what research or development
  has taken place since conception.
- Thoroughly investigate the financial stability of the
  franchisor. Obtain copies of their annual report and
  accounts. If these are more than six months out of date
  ask for management accounts.

This aspect of obtaining financial information is critical. A
franchise is a partnership and therefore a two-way flow of
information is vital from the outset. If there is any
reluctance to provide these figures I would recommend you
should not proceed with the franchise. The franchisor may
well give a good reason why the information is not
available. At the very least, however, it casts doubt upon the
management information system in place.

Now that you are getting close to a final decision, at
least on the one franchise to evaluate further, this is the
time to take up specific references. Obtain details of the
franchisor's bankers and ask your bank to take up a
reference. Also ask the franchisor for details of all existing
franchisees and not just a select few. This will give you the
opportunity of making your own selection of who you talk
to rather than talking to franchisees who may be star
performers.

If the franchisor shows any signs of reluctance in
allowing you to talk to other franchisees, apart from a
limited number of names, you need to exercise caution.
There can never be a good reason for this, the franchisor

should be willing for you to talk to any of their franchisees. Again, my advice would be to walk away from the potential franchise.

*The importance of adequate research into the background and success rate of the franchisor cannot be stressed strongly enough. As with all goods offered for sale, remember the maxim:* caveat emptor — *let the buyer beware.*

 **OBTAINING A SECOND OPINION**

Gaining an opinion on the franchisor from existing franchisees is just as important as gaining the background on the franchise. The only way that you can do this is to *talk to a sample of franchisees.* Do not restrict the sample to your immediate local area. Talk to as many as you can throughout the country in different demographic locations. For example you can, I am sure, compare your own location with a similar one elsewhere in the UK. You must go beyond this and talk to franchisees in totally different socio-economic circumstances in order to compare performance.

There are a number of questions that you need to ask existing franchisees to help you select the best franchise for you. Many of these will test the answers and information already given to you by the franchisor. The purpose of these is to *prevent any unwanted shocks* after you complete your purchase. The following are not intended to comprise an exhaustive list but merely serve as a starting point for your investigation:

● Was the initial investment sufficient to start the business or were there any unforeseen costs? Was the expenditure on equipment adequate or was further equipment required?

- How accurate were the franchisor's estimates of sales income and costs? Were the gross profit and net profit margins on target?
- Did the initial cash flow forecasts match actual cashflow and was the break-even point established correctly?
- Is the business providing the anticipated level of income?
- Is the operations manual easy to understand and follow? Are there any suggested amendments or additions that could be made?
- Was the level of training adequate and was it given at the right time? Did it prepare you sufficiently to run the franchise from the outset?
- Was the help, guidance and backup from the franchisor exactly as promised?
- Are the products or services of the quality and standard that was expected?
- Have there been any disagreements with the franchisor? If so, what did they relate to and how have they been resolved?
- If something has gone wrong how quickly has the franchisor acted to help?
- With the benefit of hindsight is there anything that they would change in the original contract?
- Overall, how satisfied are the franchisees with the way the franchise has operated. Has it met or exceeded their expectations?

There is one further aspect to take into account if you are considering the purchase of an *existing franchise operation* from a franchisee, rather than a new franchise from the franchisor. You must thoroughly investigate the reasons for the sale and accept whether the reasons are valid. In buying an existing franchise you will only be told the good points about the operation. Anything detrimental to the potential sale will more than likely remain hidden.

### Making personal observations

This makes the question of comparison between franchisees in similar demographic locations even more important. One method of investigation when buying an existing operation is *personal observation*. Make sure that you spend some considerable time, on different days and at different times of the day, observing the number of customers who visit the site. Conduct your own personal market research with a customer survey and ask questions of the people who visit the site. The franchise owner should have no objection to such investigations. If they do, this should be giving you warning signs.

*Talking to people who have already invested in the franchise concept is crucial.*

However, do understand that different franchisees may have differing opinions on the franchise. The important aspect is balance. It could be that the franchise concept works well but the franchisee does not have the skills to make it succeed. The final selection is yours and you need to choose wisely.

**KEY POINTS**

✓ Obtain a copy of the latest *Franchise World* magazine together with the *Annual Franchise Directory* to be clear on the franchise options available.

✓ Undertake your own market research as though you were starting in business in the same field.

✓ Make a short list of two, preferably three, franchise options to investigate further.

✓ Thoroughly investigate the background to the franchisor and make sure that all your questions are answered. If information is not forthcoming – be on your guard.

✓ Talk to as many existing franchisees as possible. Their opinions may differ in small ways but overall they must be satisfied with the franchise.

# 3 Evaluating the Franchise

*When evaluating the franchise you must consider two separate aspects. Is the franchise right for me, and am I right for the franchise?*

**3**

things that
really matter

1 **CONSIDERING WHETHER IT IS RIGHT FOR YOU**

2 **CHECKING VIABILITY**

3 **UNDERSTANDING THE CONTRACT**

A good franchisor will not accept just anyone as a franchisee. Just as you will be concerned at evaluating the franchise, the franchisor will be concerned as to whether you are acceptable to them.

A reputable franchisor will be looking for people who have the capability to *run their own business and succeed*. Any failures within a franchise will affect the reputation of the franchisor as well as the individual franchisees. Having asked the searching questions of the franchisor you have selected you can, and indeed should, expect the same questioning into your own background and experience. If you do not encounter such an investigation you should perhaps again be on your guard. The franchisor should be aiming for you to succeed for their benefit as well as yours.

### IS THIS YOU?

**(?)** ● *I'm not sure I have all the skills to run a business but the franchisor says that they provide all training.* ● *The franchisor wants to see me at home to meet my family, what have they got to do with it?* ● *Will I need an accountant to prepare any figures?* ● *Do I really need expensive lawyers, the contract is not that complicated?*

## **(1)   CONSIDERING WHETHER IT IS RIGHT FOR YOU**

One of the key points to remember when you are looking at a franchise is that you are taking the first step to being self-employed. There is really no difference between buying a franchise and starting your own business. There may be advantages in a franchise in that the concept has been tried and tested but it still means you will be *working for yourself*. You will not be an employee of the franchisor despite the fact that they may tell you how to operate the business. So before proceeding you must satisfy yourself that you have the necessary skills to run a business.

There may be many reasons why you are contemplating buying a franchise. You may have become tired of working for someone else, or perhaps you are looking for a career change, or a fresh start following redundancy. You have probably been used to doing your job whilst the management of the business went on around you.

*Buying a franchise means that it will now be your responsibility to run your business. Make sure that you are ready for this.*

If you have a family you will also require strong support. Working for yourself is not an easy option. It will require hard work with the probability of long hours. Paid holidays and days off sick will be a thing of the past. Weekends will also probably be encroached upon to deal with basic administration. All of these things need to be thought through first and *discussed with your family*. Unless you have their support you will be fighting to survive on two separate fronts, at home and at work.

Another important aspect to consider when evaluating the franchise is the degree to which you think you will *enjoy the work*. Unless you are enthusiastic about the work there is little point in buying a franchise. You must consider the franchise opportunity as a chance to do something you want to do. It should be a natural progression in your chosen career path.

## Considering your personal characteristics

You also need to consider your own personal characteristics. It is accepted by franchisors and established franchisees alike that the most important characteristics are as follows:

- management ability
- willingness to work hard
- desire to succeed.

The question to ask yourself is – *do I have these characteristics?*

Management ability is of prime importance and the theory can be gained through study. Practical ability, however, can only be gained through experience. If you do not have both the *willingness to work hard* and the *desire to succeed* you should not be considering franchising.

The prospective franchisor will be looking for all these characteristics and you may be subjected to a rigorous background check. In some cases they may prefer you to have no knowledge or experience of the market in which they operate. This is on the basis that full training will be provided and they would prefer you not to have any preconceptions. On the other hand, as in the example of the mobile car mechanic, prior experience is essential. It will depend on the stance of the individual franchisor.

The franchisor may also require to meet you, at least once, in your home environment. This will be done to investigate two aspects of your background:

- They will want to gauge the support and commitment of your whole family to the business venture.
- They will also be looking for signs of organisation and tidiness. People who live in a sloppy and disorganised manner are likely to run a business in the same fashion.

A further consideration for the franchisor is *your personal means*. They will require confirmation that you can afford the franchise and, if necessary, have additional money should anything go wrong. It is just as important to them as it is to you that you succeed. It will not just be the initial fee that they are interested in. They are also looking to you to provide them with an income from your business.

*A franchise is an ongoing partnership relationship and as such you have to be suitable for each other. If you do not get along together on a personal basis, it is unlikely that you will make good business partners.*

 ## CHECKING VIABILITY

When considering the purchase of a franchise you need to make the same assessment of viability as you would of buying an existing business. The only difference is that with a franchise there are two aspects of viability to consider. Not only do you need to check the *viability of the franchise,* you also need to check the *viability of the franchisor.*

Confidence in the financial stability of the franchisor is essential. They must have the resources to enable them to perform their contractual obligations. You will also want to be assured that your investment in the franchise is remunerative. Having reached this stage of the selection and evaluation process you now need professional help. You need to engage a qualified accountant to assist with the assessment of the financial viability of the franchise.

During the selection process you should already have gained the financial accounts of the franchisor. These need to be analysed by the accountant who should then prepare a report on the *general financial health* of the franchisor. The report must look specifically at the *long-term prospects* of the franchisor. If there is any likelihood that the franchisor will not be in business in the foreseeable future there is little chance that you will succeed. Once you are satisfied on this extremely important point you can then move on to the next stage – investigating the viability of the proposed franchise operation.

At this point remember that you are not looking at the viability of the initial franchise fee. This will be a one-off payment and will not feature yet in any part of your investigation. What you will be looking at is the *underlying viability of the business* and whether it can *provide you with a satisfactory income*.

A good franchisor will maintain management financial information on all their franchisees and will provide you with forecast figures for your new franchise. Unlike starting your own business, you will not be expected to prepare the projections yourself. Whilst this does have initial benefits, the projections, if accepted by you, will be used later if you need to raise finance. It is therefore essential that you have a thorough understanding of what these projections represent. Initially, the important part is to satisfy yourself on three points:

- Are the figures reasonable taking into account the location?
- Can the figures be achieved?
- Are the timings included in the forecasts realistic?

Having already spoken to existing franchisees you may be able to obtain confirmation from them of the validity of the figures. On the other hand they may be unwilling to give you details of their own performance. At the very least, they will hopefully provide you with details of the accounting ratios that they achieve. These should give you confirmation of the *gross and net profit margins*. Make sure that you use the services of your accountant to complete the analysis.

You should also use your accountant to check the accuracy of the forecasts in terms of the timing of statutory payments such as VAT, National Insurance contributions, and personal tax under PAYE. With their local knowledge they can also assess whether standard costs such as business rates, electricity and water costs are reasonable.

Another useful resource for evaluating the forecasts will be your bank manager. At this stage you should make it clear that you are not putting a funding proposition to the bank but are seeking their expertise in assessing the forecasts. As previously mentioned the bank will have a specialist franchising section which may well have had prior dealings with the franchisor in question. They may be able to give advice on whether the forecasts are reasonable, taking into account the historic performance of other franchisees on their books.

### Studying profit and cash

There are two important features of the forecasts that should be studied carefully: *profit* and *cash*. It is vital that you do not confuse the two. Profit is essential to the long-term viability of your business. Cash is essential to short-term viability. Remember, profit is a paper figure only, until you actually receive the cash it means nothing.

For example, you sell goods to a customer for £100. They cost you £50 to purchase so a profit of £50 has been made. However, you allow your customer to pay after 30 days' credit. Whilst you have made the sale, and the technical profit, you have not actually received the cash. Your customer then cannot pay for the goods which by now have been used. You have therefore made a loss of £50, being the cost of the goods to you in the first place. Your paper profit of £50 has been turned into a debt of £50.

*Cash is the life blood of a business. It continues in a cycle – out to pay for goods and in from your customers. Profit is a paper exercise. Without cash there will be no profit. Viability of a business can only be achieved with positive cash flow.*

## ③ UNDERSTANDING THE CONTRACT

As with all commercial contracts, the *terms and conditions* relating to the franchise will be extremely complex. You must engage the services of a lawyer from the outset, preferably one who has experience of franchising. Be clear on one thing, sign absolutely nothing until you have received legal advice. The services of a good lawyer will not come cheap but they could save you from entering into something you do not understand.

The terms and conditions in the contract will vary from franchise to franchise. They should, however, cover the following factors:

- The cost of the franchise.
- The location and territorial rights.
- The property and equipment requirement.
- The operation of the franchise.
- Renewal and termination conditions.

The first three of these all relate to exactly what you are getting for your money and are covered in greater detail in Chapter 4. The operational aspect of the franchise, and the renewal and termination conditions, will impose contractual obligations on you that will be unrelated to the fee that you will pay.

The *operational aspects* of the franchise will cover the rights of both the franchisor and the franchisee within the business. Factors that you need to look for include:

- The degree of control the franchisor has over you.
- The management assistance, training and development to be provided by the franchisor.
- The management information system to be implemented, including accounting and reporting requirements.
- The goods or services to be supplied and whether they can only be purchased through the franchisor. Any restrictions on what can be sold or supplied by you.
- The hours the business will trade.
- The advertising arrangements for the franchise on a national or local level and the allocation of costs in this respect.

The conditions relating to the *renewal and termination* of the franchise will usually look at four scenarios:

- Renewal of the franchise option for a further period. All franchises are only available for a limited period of time, the average being seven years. It is important that, if you so wish, you have the automatic right of renewal. In some cases a further fee will be payable and if so this must be clearly defined.

- Sale of the business by you. The franchisor will be likely to want first option to buy if you decide to sell. The franchisor will also insist on a right of veto over any other potential purchaser to ensure that they are acceptable. You must also be aware of the likely consequences in the unfortunate circumstances of your death or permanent disability.
- Termination of the franchise by you. A minimum period will be given before you may terminate the agreement. The franchise fee will be forfeited and there may be other financial penalties. For example you may have to compensate the franchisor in respect of loss of income. There may also be conditions imposed on the sale of existing stock and equipment.
- Termination of the franchise by the franchisor. Any breach of the franchise agreement could lead to termination of the agreement by the franchisor. You need to be aware of the circumstances that could lead to such action. The agreement should also specify any period of time you will be allowed to remedy any breach of the agreement.

You need to have a great understanding of the terms and conditions relating to this final scenario. Whilst the franchisor would only take such a step as a final resort you must be aware that the agreement will undoubtedly be in their favour. You must make sure that you *understand all the penalties* that could be imposed on you for non-performance of the agreement.

*It is highly unlikely that the franchisor will agree to change or negotiate any of the terms and conditions of the agreement. They should be the same for all franchisees. Once the agreement is signed you will be committed. Make sure you take time to fully understand the commitment you are undertaking.*

### KEY POINTS

✓ Satisfy yourself that you have the skills and characteristics to run your own business.

✓ Make sure that the franchisor is financially stable and able to commit the resources required to assist you in running the franchise.

✓ Use the services of a qualified accountant to thoroughly investigate the validity of the financial forecasts provided to you by the franchisor.

✓ Use the assistance of your bank's franchising section which may have details of the performance of existing franchisees.

✓ Engage the services of a commercial lawyer who has experience of franchising to help you fully understand the franchise agreement.

✓ Do not sign any document until you have received professional advice and you are completely sure you fully understand what it is you are signing.

# 4 Assessing the Cost

*You must be clear on the true cost of the franchise, not just the initial fee, and know exactly what you will receive in exchange.*

**4**

things that
really matter

1 **ESTABLISHING THE INITIAL COST**

2 **CONSIDERING THE ONGOING COSTS**

3 **APPRECIATING WHAT YOU GET FOR YOUR MONEY**

4 **RAISING THE MONEY**

When assessing the cost remember that the franchise does not just involve an up-front fee. There will also be *ongoing royalty payments* as well as potential *renewal fees*.

The franchise will only be available to you *under licence for a limited period*. During that time you must achieve a suitable return on your initial investment to make the franchise financially viable to you. Apart from making a satisfactory living from the venture you must aim to recoup the initial investment or it merely becomes a wasting asset.

Compare your investment in the franchise to making a deposit in a building society. Whilst invested in the account you expect to receive interest on your money. At the end of the fixed term you can then withdraw the money from the account. In the case of the franchise the interest comes from the profits of the business. The important part to remember is that *your initial investment must also be recouped from the profits* of the business. It will not be returned to you by the franchisor upon the expiry of the franchise licence.

## IS THIS YOU?

● Once I've paid the franchise fee that's it isn't it?
● All the costs seem straightforward but I'm not happy with these management charges. ● I'm really lucky I've got just enough to buy the franchise of my dreams. ● It's brilliant, everything I need is included, all I have to do now is find a property. ● I don't need to borrow much, the forecasts the franchisor has given me show only a small overdraft.

*A franchise might be a safer alternative than starting your own business but there is a price to pay. You are working for yourself but the franchisor will still take their ongoing fees regardless of whether you make a profit or not.*

## ① ESTABLISHING THE INITIAL COST

The amount of the initial cost will depend on two factors: whether the franchise fee is solely for the business concept or whether it also includes all the equipment necessary to trade. In the majority of cases the up-front fee will represent 10 per cent of the total start-up costs. This fee will only relate to the sale by the franchisor of the business concept. It still leaves you to *finance the required premises and equipment.*

This means that the total start-up costs for each franchise will vary from franchise to franchise depending on location. In some of the more complex franchise deals the franchisor will acquire and equip the property for a franchisee. However, there may still be a difference in the total cost of the franchise relating to the cost of the property.

The franchisor may also opt for a small fee initially but a larger percentage as an ongoing royalty. Conversely there may be a large up-front fee and reduced ongoing costs. It will depend on how the franchisor wishes to recoup their costs. Some will reduce the initial financial start-up burden on the basis that their costs, together with a profit, will be paid over time by way of the royalty payments.

Whichever option the franchisor chooses it is important to understand that the initial fee may only represent a *small proportion* of the total start-up costs. Within the financial forecasts already provided to you there could be a large element of *capital expenditure*. This must be taken into account when establishing the initial cost. A further factor will be whether you can finance the entire start-up costs from your own resources.

If you are having to borrow money to finance the purchase there will be further costs involved, certainly by way of interest payments and probably bank fees. These will all add to the overall cost of the franchise. At this stage you may need to rework the cashflow forecast taking into account your own capital injection together with any loans.

It is vital that you understand that the initial cost does not just relate to the franchise fee. A substantial sum will be required to actually start the business. Do not forget that there will also be accountant and lawyer fees to be paid.

*All too often new businesses start with insufficient capital. Whatever the start-up costs are estimated at, a further margin of at least 10 per cent would be prudent. A reserve must be in the background just in case something goes wrong.*

 **CONSIDERING THE ONGOING COSTS**

There are a number of different terms for the ongoing costs:

- management fees
- service charges
- royalties.

There are also two main methods of calculation, either based upon a *percentage of turnover* or a *fixed monthly fee*. In some cases a *minimum level of fee* is also imposed. The most common method of calculation is on a percentage of turnover and you can expect to pay between 5 per cent and 10 per cent. This is regarded as the fairest method of charging. It means that you know exactly what you will have to pay and it can be calculated relatively easily. From the franchisor's point of view it means that they will also benefit from the growth in your business.

There could also be the prospect of the franchisor gaining two profit streams from you. If, as part of the franchise agreement, you can only sell products bought from the franchisor, they will also be gaining profits on those sales. The franchisor will then gain a further payment when you sell the products to your customers. In this sort of circumstance it is usual for there to be a reduced percentage fee. In overall terms, however, the ongoing payments to the franchisor should therefore remain broadly the same.

When assessing the ongoing costs you need to exercise extreme caution in order to ensure that you *include all prospective costs*. In some cases there may be expenditure on advertising which is charged separately and held in a central fund by the franchisor. In other cases, the franchisor may insist that you allocate a percentage of your budget for your own advertising. In all cases, the franchisor will insist on having control over the advertising content.

The important consideration for ongoing fees is to satisfy yourself that they are fair and that you cannot be exploited by the franchisor. These fees are to pay for the ongoing assistance of the franchisor and they must relate clearly to the perceived value of that assistance.

The franchisor will want a steady income stream to pay for the ongoing costs of providing assistance to you. The franchisor should remember that these fees must be reasonable and allow you to make your own profit.

*Long-term growth can only come about with growth in both the franchisor's and the franchisee's businesses.*

 ### APPRECIATING WHAT YOU GET FOR YOUR MONEY

What you will get for your money will depend upon the individual franchise package. Remember that you are also buying a business concept and image and therefore you will also be paying for intangible *good will*. In the most basic franchise package there will be two key elements:

- The brand name and image – a licence to trade under the name of the franchisor in a specified location and for a determinate period.
- Practical training together with an operations manual – full training in how to conduct the business. The operations manual will outline the procedures and methods to be followed in running the franchise.

The franchise package should include the granting of a licence by the franchisor to you to use the brand name and image in your own business. This will be for a limited period of time and the terms and conditions of renewal should be clearly defined. It must also contain exclusive territorial rights with an undertaking by the franchisor not to sell a further franchise within a defined area.

The package will also include details of the products or services to be sold and whether or not they must be purchased from the franchisor. If the franchisor is a manufacturer, with you operating a retail outlet, there can be no doubt that the franchisor will only allow the sale of their own goods. Even if the franchisor themselves are retailers it is likely they will insist upon being your only supplier. This could actually be to your advantage. The franchisor may have negotiated substantial discounts with their own suppliers for bulk purchases that should, at least in part, be passed on to you.

### Understanding the operations manual

For a franchise in a service industry the *operations manual* will form the most valuable asset of the franchise package. It will contain, in small detail, the procedures and methods to be adopted in running the business. It will be provided to you as part of your initial training and should equip you with all the required skills to operate the franchise. It will also outline the financial and other reporting requirements for the management information system operated by the franchisor. As part of your assessment you must make sure that you fully understand the operations manual. You should at the same time establish how often it is updated and indeed when the version that you will be given was published.

### The turnkey

In a slightly more complex franchise package, the equipment required or an opening amount of stock will also be included. It is possible, although normally only in the most expensive of franchises, that the necessary trading premises will also be supplied, fully fitted and ready to trade. This sort of package is called a **turnkey**. Effectively the keys are handed over from the franchisor to the franchisee upon payment of the fee and the business can start immediately.

## Obtaining equipment

If equipment is required by the franchise, two options might form part of the package:

- The franchisor will provide everything required.
- Details of the equipment required will be given by the franchisor, leaving you free to arrange the purchase yourself.

With the first option the franchisor will arrange the purchase of all desired equipment that will then be sold to you. It is possible that if the franchisor is a large business they will be able to negotiate discounts on the deal. Whether these are passed on to you will of course depend on the franchisor. They will no doubt in any event charge a mark-up on the purchase cost to make a profit themselves.

With the second option the franchisor will provide you with detailed specifications of the equipment, leaving you to purchase the items yourself. In some cases they may be extremely specific in terms of make and model and in others they may leave the decision to you.

Take as an example the franchise of a printing business. The basic layout, design and format of the actual basic shop will be clearly defined to comply with the brand image. The equipment, however, may be left to your choice giving you the opportunity to purchase the most up to date systems. On the other hand, the franchisor may already have a deal with an equipment supplier and you may be forced to purchase specific machines, either direct or through the franchisor.

As an alternative, some franchisors arrange for all the necessary equipment to be leased by the franchisee. This means that whilst the equipment is not yours it does reduce the overall start-up cost. You will still need to take into account the cost of the monthly leasing payment.

### Receiving value for money

All the above factors relate to what you will get for your initial franchise fee. The final part of your assessment is to establish exactly what assistance and support you will receive for the ongoing management charges. There will be three factors involved:

- advertising
- administrative support
- ongoing training and development.

In each case you need to satisfy yourself that you will receive *value for money*. All of these factors may, however, have to be taken on trust at the outset. It is worthwhile talking to other established franchisees to gain their opinion on the quality and standard of the after sales support.

*Contractual obligations can be difficult to enforce, especially where the franchisor is not carrying out their responsibilities. The franchise agreement will always give the franchisor greater rights against the franchisee for non-performance than the other way around.*

 **RAISING THE MONEY**

Now that you have established the true total cost of buying the franchise you obviously need to consider *where that money is going to come from*. The first place will be from your own resources, either from existing savings or other assets that can be sold to realise cash. As with all business propositions you need to invest a significant percentage into the cost of the venture before external funders such as banks will consider lending you money. At the very least you will need to provide 20 per cent of the total funding requirement from your own resources.

The advantages that you will have in raising funds to

purchase the franchise are twofold:

- You are buying a business that has been well tried and tested and has a proven concept.
- Because the major banks have specialist franchising sections they may already have an understanding of the historic performance of other franchises granted by the same franchisor.

Under normal circumstances, assuming that you need to borrow money to fund the purchase, the funding package that you will require will have three components:

- your own capital investment
- an overdraft facility for working capital
- a loan for capital expenditure.

The *overdraft* will be required to finance the short-term element as revealed by the cash flow forecast that has been prepared. In effect this finances the day to day running of the business. It covers the time taken to receive payment from your customers from the time of the initial sale. This will obviously only relate to sales on credit. The overdraft should fluctuate from debit to credit and this is the most cost-effective way of short-term borrowing. You are only paying interest on the days when you are overdrawn.

A *loan* may be required for the capital expenditure element of the franchise. This will relate to the purchase of the property and equipment. This is long-term finance but you should be aware that the funder will normally link the period of the loan to the period of the franchise. For example, if the franchise licence has initially been granted for a period of seven years, the loan will also be granted over a maximum period of seven years.

The reasons for this are that the funder cannot be sure

that the license will be renewed, or indeed that you will want to seek renewal. The loan therefore needs to be paid back before the franchise is terminated. This is quite a reasonable requirement. In any event you should be looking to *pay back all the initial start-up costs over the period of the franchise*. If you do renew the licence at the expiry of the initial term there may well be a further fee involved which may require a new loan.

### KEY POINTS

✓ Make sure you establish the true total start-up costs of the franchise.

✓ Be clear on how the ongoing costs are calculated and when they are to be paid to the franchisor.

✓ Evaluate carefully and have a clear understanding of exactly what you are getting for your investment.

✓ Ensure that the ongoing support provided by the franchisor is clearly defined and that it represents value for money.

✓ Take the advice of your bank when putting together the funding package. Now that you are going to be self-employed there will be numerous other factors they can help you consider.

# 5 And After You've Bought the Franchise?

*A new partnership has been formed. Welcome to the world of franchising. This is where the hard work starts.*

**3**

**things that really matter**

1 **MANAGING THE ONGOING RELATIONSHIP**

2 **UNDERSTANDING THE RESPONSIBILITIES OF EACH PARTY**

3 **AVOIDING FAILURE**

Having undertaken your research and satisfied yourself on the franchise's viability, you signed the contract. It is important that you understand *what happens now* that you are about to run your own business as a franchisee.

The whole foundation of the franchise concept relies upon a positive partnership approach and the ongoing franchisee/franchisor relationship should be open. Discuss any problems at an early stage before they get out of hand. Remember that the franchisor will want you to succeed. Even if there are few other franchisees in your region, the franchisor should have considerable experience of any potential problems. *You are paying for ongoing support* and you should have no hesitation in asking for help.

The responsibilities will be clearly defined in the contract and must be adhered to by both parties. If they can perform their obligations without further reference to the contract until renewal the relationship will strengthen and grow.

### IS THIS YOU?

• *Now that I'm a franchisee nothing can go wrong. The franchisor will always be there for me.* • *I didn't appreciate all the paperwork that would be involved, why does the franchisor require so much information on my business?* • *I don't like it when the franchisor visits me, he always seems to find problems.* • *I'm not receiving the support that I should be, if I don't get it why should I pay for it?*

*As soon as one party starts to use the contract as a weapon the relationship is over and failure of the business will probably follow. You must work together to succeed.*

### MANAGING THE ONGOING RELATIONSHIP

An essential element of the ongoing relationship will be *communication*. This must be a two-way process. A good franchisor will have a well developed system of communication with specific people for you to contact within their business. Contact between you and the franchisor will take place in three basic forms:

- personal visits
- written communications
- franchise meetings.

Personal contact between the parties plays an important part in the relationship. It will usually be conducted by the franchisor themselves or by specialist support staff. It is essential to the franchisor that you quickly become one of the team and in the early days of the relationship a high level of personal support will be required. The first element of the franchise will of course be training in the systems and methods of the franchise and this should be carried out on a *personal basis*.

The franchisor will also want to be sure that you are operating the franchise correctly. At the outset the *personal visits* will be extremely regular to ensure compliance with the operating standards and contractual obligations. You must not view these visits as being intrusive. They are designed to help you and you must take full advantage of them. The franchisor has designed the systems and procedures to work efficiently. If you are not using them correctly you are only making the business more difficult for yourself.

*Written communications* from the franchisor will probably be extensive. Quite apart from normal correspondence, these may include regular newsletters and updates to the operations manual. Written communications will also be required from you on a frequent basis. These will include the regular financial and other returns required by the franchisor for their management information system. Make sure that you understand exactly what is required.

Most franchisors will also hold *regular meetings* of all their franchisees. Depending on the overall size of the franchise these could be on a regional or a national basis. These will give you an opportunity to meet other franchisees and are a very effective way of networking. They give you a chance to discuss your concerns and problems with others and learn from their ideas.

These meetings will also give the franchisor an opportunity to keep you up to date with developments within the business. You have a right to be kept informed of what is happening in the overall franchise operation and these meetings will help to strengthen the bond between franchisor and franchisee.

### Working in partnership

A further essential element to the ongoing relationship is the monitoring and support provided by the franchisor. The monitoring system imposed by the franchisor must be seen to be fair to both parties. For you as franchisee it will be important that the system does not pose an overburden on your administrative work. For the franchisor it needs to provide sufficient information to monitor your performance and check that the correct management charges are calculated.

The ongoing support that you receive will take many forms. Training programmes are of course essential to keep you up to date. You will also want to know what market research is being undertaken and be informed of the advertising and promotion campaigns planned by the franchisor. You will also want details of the research and development of new products.

This support process should also be two-way. If you need help you must ask for it. If you can provide feedback to the franchisor that has been given to you by your customers on the products or services you should do so.

*A franchise is a partnership and it is vital to ensure that both parties manage the relationship in a positive and constructive manner.*

 **UNDERSTANDING THE RESPONSIBILITIES OF EACH PARTY**

Both you and the franchisor have clear and distinct *responsibilities*. They could be likened to that of parent and child. The franchisor, as parent, has responsibility for you as the franchisee, as a child, certainly in the early years. It is for the franchisor to pass on to you the necessary skills and knowledge to enable you to succeed.

The responsibilities in the assessment process are also mutual. It is for the franchisor to satisfy themselves that you would be a suitable franchisee. As potential franchisee it is for you to satisfy yourself that the franchise is right for you.

## The franchisor's responsibilities

Even before the franchisor can offer the franchise to you it is their obvious responsibility to have tested the concept and proved that it will work. This will need to be done with at least one pilot operation. Once that has been established it is for the franchisor to put together a suitable package that can be sold to potential franchisees.

It is then the franchisor's responsibility to ensure that suitable *training* is given to franchisees. The quality of the training is a key factor. This must equip you with all the skills necessary to make the franchise a success. The franchisor will also need to provide the back-up and support services that will be detailed within the contract.

These will include the responsibilities for advertising which, together with product development and design, are key areas to the success of both franchisor and franchisee.

When looking at the responsibilities of the franchisor it is important that they are members of the British Franchise Association. Being a member requires the franchisor to abide by the published Code of Ethics. Whilst hopefully your relationship will not come under strain this does at least provide you with some form of protection. It will also give you access to a formal arbitration scheme should there be any dispute that cannot be resolved between yourself and the franchisor.

### The franchisee's responsibilities

As franchisee you have a number of responsibilities.

- You have a responsibility to yourself to correctly evaluate the franchise.
- You must be objective and honest with yourself in the assessment of your own skills to run a franchise.
- You must draw up the short list of potential franchisors yourself and meet with them personally to discuss the opportunities available.
- You must accept that franchising will impose constraints on the way that you run your business.
- You must abide by the contents of the operations manual and not try to take any shortcuts in the operational method that you may consider to be more appropriate.
- You have a responsibility to provide the franchisor with feedback from 'grass roots' operations that may assist with the further development of the franchise itself.
- You have a responsibility to the franchisor to run the franchise in a proper manner. You must not do anything that could damage the image or brand of the franchise.
- You are obliged to supply the management information required by the franchisor in an accurate and timely manner.
- You are bound to pay the correct management fees as and when they fall due.

*Both parties have a primary responsibility to be completely open and honest in their dealings with each other. Right from the beginning of the relationship it is important that mutual trust is gained.*

**AVOIDING FAILURE**

The risk of a franchise failing is statistically lower than that of other start-up businesses. That does not mean that you can afford to be complacent. There are still risks involved and in many ways they can be more complicated. They are also doubled in number. Not only is there the risk of your business failing but the additional risk that *the franchisor themselves could fail.*

There are any number of reasons why a franchisor can fail, examples of which include:

- The franchise operation may be badly structured.
- There may have been insufficient research and testing of the pilot operation.
- The franchise may have been expanded too quickly, leading to the franchisor having inadequate resources to provide support.
- The franchisor may lack the management ability to run the franchise.

You must therefore not only manage your own business but at the same time look for any warning signs in your dealings with the franchisor that the operation itself is failing. The franchisor is contractually bound to provide management and support services and if the quality of these deteriorate you must not hesitate to investigate.

What you must not do, under any circumstances, is withhold payment of the management charges. This would immediately place you in breach of contract. A franchise operation is a partnership. It is better to talk to the franchisor to try to help resolve the problem. If the franchisor fails this will have an impact on all franchisees. The brand and image of the franchise may be tarnished.

The whole concept of franchising is based on a *proven image and brand*. In the event of failure these could be the only remaining assets of the franchisor. They still remain vital to you as franchisee. Depending on the size of the franchise it may be that a sufficient number of franchisees can step in and buy the franchise concept from the franchisor. This will at least allow the franchisees to continue to trade with minimal disruption whilst the management and support services are reorganised.

The potential failure of the franchisor is just one side of the equation. Your own business will still face the normal risks of failure. There are many reasons why businesses fail but some of the most common include:

- insufficient start-up capital
- not making enough sales
- setting an incorrect price
- rising overhead costs
- poor accounting and control systems
- pure bad management
- bad debts
- health problems.

As a franchisee you may have no control over some of these, for example pricing decisions. Problems of one form or another *will* occur. It is essential that you recognise the *cause of the problem*, as opposed to the symptom, and take corrective action. Treating the symptom rather than the cause will only bring temporary relief. It is more than likely that the problem will recur.

As soon as you encounter any problems it is in your own best interests to consult the franchisor. Other franchisees may have encountered similar problems and, based on their experiences, there may be good contingency plans in place.

You can only benefit from these if you *advise the franchisor* at the earliest possible stage.

*Once you have purchased a franchise it becomes your business. Whilst the franchisor will be there in the background to offer assistance you still face the same risks of failure. Understand these risks, and what can be done to avoid them, and you have a greater chance of success.*

### KEY POINTS

✓ Always be open and honest in all your dealings with the franchisor. You expect the same from them and they have every right to expect it of you.

✓ Take advantage of the regular visits from the franchisor to help improve your business.

✓ Make sure that you understand the extent and timing of the management information the franchisor requires from you.

✓ If the quality and timing of the management support supplied by the franchisor deteriorates in any way make an immediate investigation.

✓ Contact the franchisor at the earliest opportunity in the event of problems. They are there to help you, make sure you use them.

# The British Franchise Association

The British Franchise Association (BFA) was formed in 1977 and is the single regulatory body for franchising in the UK. It is a non-profit making organisation responsible for developing and promoting fair and ethical franchising through its member franchisor companies.

The BFA was established to:

- Develop and continuously improve standards of good practice in franchising.
- Accredit franchisors who meet those standards.
- Promote good franchising as represented by accredited franchisors to the general public, the business community, government, and the media.
- Provide to the general public as prospective franchisees information and education to help them make effective judgements in choosing the best franchise for them.

The BFA have a number of publications which can help prospective franchisees and you are strongly encouraged to contact them for help. Their main publications are:

**The BFA Franchisee Information Pack** – priced at £29.00. The pack includes:

- A full list of BFA member companies, what they do, contact details, investment costs and other relevant information.
- A free CD ROM.
- A list of affiliate advisers which include solicitors, chartered accountants, banks, franchise consultants and insurance brokers who all have specialist knowledge of franchising.
- Details of the BFA's role in franchising.
- Information on forthcoming franchise exhibitions.

- Advice and guidance on the laws and ethics relating to franchising.
- A free copy of *Business Franchise Magazine* and *Franchise Link Magazine*.

**Introduction to Franchising Video** – priced at £9.95.
The video provides a thirty minute introduction to the world of franchising from the people with first hand experience. Included are interviews with BFA franchisor members and their franchisees together with advice from professional advisers. The video covers:

- What is franchising?
- What are the benefits?
- How to become a franchisor or franchisee.
- Who are the franchisors?
- An introduction to the work of the BFA.
- How to get further information.

**The BFA Annual Survey of Franchising** – priced at £87.50.
Whilst somewhat expensive the annual survey could be a worthwhile investment because it provides a detailed analysis of franchising in the UK. The survey contents include:

- Industry size and dynamics including turnover, employment and future expectations.
- Character of franchising in the UK – top performing sectors, growth areas, progress and prospects, regional distribution of franchising.
- Profile characteristics of franchisees which include the characteristics looked for by franchisors, the ideal profile of a franchisee applicant and action taken prior to acquiring a franchise.

- Report and analysis of franchise charges including franchise fees, start-up costs and recurring franchise costs.
- Franchise performance data and analysis including opportunities and changes in the next twelve months.
- Essential information on marketing, recruitment, new business opportunities, network growth and performance.

The BFA have also exclusively endorsed two CD ROMs, CDfex and Franchise Adviser which help prospective franchisees search for the right BFA member franchise opportunity. Both of these are available from: http://www.whichfranchise.com.

Further details can be obtained from:
The British Franchise Association
Thames View
Newtown Road
Henley on Thames
Oxon.
RG9 1HG
Tel: (01491) 578050
Fax: (01491) 573517
http://www.british-franchise.org.uk

# Useful Addresses

Business Franchise Directory
Miller Freeman
Blenheim House
630 Chiswick High Road
London W4 5BG
Tel: (020) 8742 2828

Franchise World Magazine
James House
37 Nottingham Road
London SW17 7EA
Tel: (020) 8767 1371
http://www.franchiseworld.co.uk

The Franchise Business
18 Chilsdown Way
Purbrook
Hants PO7 5DT
Tel: (023) 9225 8111
Fax: (023) 9225 8777
http://www.franchisebusiness.co.uk

The National Franchise Exhibition
http://www.nfe.co.uk

Phil Stone
Parkstone Management Consultancy
9 Parkstone Close
Hastings Hill
Sunderland
Tyne and Wear SR4 9PA
http://www.pkstone.demon.co.uk

For general advice and guidance on running your own business contact your local Business Link – telephone the national help line for details of the nearest office – 0345 567765 or search on the website http:///www.businesslink.co.uk